AMERICAN HEROES

# SACAGAWEA

*Brave Shoshone Girl*

# American Heroes

# Sacagawea
## *Brave Shoshone Girl*

SNEED B. COLLARD III

**Marshall Cavendish**
Benchmark
New York

*For Vicki Spandel and Ann Marland,
true education trailblazers in the Oregon Territory*

Marshall Cavendish Benchmark
99 White Plains Road
Tarrytown, New York 10591-9001
www.marshallcavendish.us

*Library of Congress Cataloging-in-Publication Data*
Collard, Sneed B.
Sacagawea : brave Shoshone girl / by Sneed B. Collard III.
p. cm. — (American heroes)
Summary: "A juvenile biography of the courageous Shoshone woman who accompanied
the Lewis and Clark expedition"—Provided by publisher.
Includes bibliographical references and index.
ISBN-13: 978-0-7614-2166-5
ISBN-10: 0-7614-2166-1
1. Sacagawea—Juvenile literature. 2. Shoshoni women—Biography—Juvenile literature. 3. Shoshoni Indians—
Biography—Juvenile literature. 4. Lewis and Clark Expedition (1804–1806)—Juvenile literature. I. Title.
F592.7.S123C65 2006
970.004'97—dc22          2005037557

Editor: Joyce Stanton
Editorial Director: Michelle Bisson
Art Director: Anahid Hamparian
Series Designer and Compositor: Anne Scatto / PIXEL PRESS
Map by Rodica Prato
Printed in Malaysia
1  3  5  6  4  2

Images provided by Rose Corbett Gordon, Art Editor,
Mystic CT, from the following sources:
*Front cover:* David Frazier/The Image Works;
*Back cover:* Historical Picture Archive/Corbis
*Page i:* David Frazier/The Image Works; *page ii:* Walters
Art Museum, Baltimore/Bridgeman Art Library;
*page vi:* The Art Archive/Buffalo Bill Historical Center,
Cody, Wyoming; *page 3:* New-York Historical Society/
Bridgeman Art Library; *page 4:* Historical Picture
Archive/Corbis; *page 7:* The Art Archive/Gift of WJ
(Bill) Holcombe, Bear Creek Ranch, Dubois, Wyoming/
Buffalo Bill Historical Center, Cody, Wyoming;
*page 8:* Joslyn Art Museum, Omaha, Nebraska;

*pages 12 & 24:* Smithsonian American Art Museum,
Washington, DC/Art Resource, NY; *page 15:* Courtesy
Frederic Remington Art Museum, Ogdensburg, New
York; *page 16:* Painting *Lewis and Clark: The Departure
from the Wood River Encampment, May 14, 1804* by Gary
R. Lucy. Courtesy of the Gary R. Lucy Gallery, Inc.
Washington, MO, http://www.garylucy.com;
*pages 19 & 20:* Gilcrease Museum, Tulsa OK;
*page 23:* John Ford Clymer, Sacajawea at the Big Water,
© Courtesy of Mrs. John F. Clymer and the Clymer
Museum of Art; *page 27:* Travel Montana;
*page 28:* Hulton Archive/Getty Images; *page 31:* Stock
Montage; *pages 32 & 35:* James Leynse/Corbis

# CONTENTS

*Lewis and Clark's famous journey changed our nation forever.*

# Sacagawea

In 1804, a group of men set off on a great journey. They were led by Meriwether Lewis and William Clark. Between 1804 and 1806, these men traveled eight thousand miles. They explored new lands. They met new people. What they learned changed the United States forever. But without the help of one young woman, their journey might have failed. Her name was Sacagawea.

Sacagawea was a Shoshone Indian. Much of her early life is a mystery. Western American Indian tribes did not have a written language, so no one wrote about Sacagawea's childhood. We do know that she was born in about 1788. Her people lived in the northern Rocky Mountains. Today, these lands are part of Idaho and Montana.

*Sacagawea's people lived in the northern Rocky Mountains.*

*The Shoshones depended on horses to hunt bison.*

Sacagawea's people were fine horsemen. Every year, they rode out onto the plains to hunt bison. Sometimes, they fought with other tribes. To stay away from their enemies, the Shoshones spent most of the year in the mountains. Life in the mountains was hard. No bison lived there. The Shoshones struggled to find food. As a child, Sacagawea learned many skills to survive.

When Sacagawea was about eleven years old, her life turned upside down. One day, she went out to gather food with the people of her tribe. Suddenly, a band of Hidatsa Indians attacked. The Hidatsas killed several Shoshones. They kidnapped Sacagawea. They took her to a village far to the east. She became their prisoner.

*In a Hidatsa village, people take part in a religious ceremony.*

*At the age of twelve or so, Sacagawea was married to*
*fur trader Toussaint Charbonneau.*

As a prisoner of the Hidatsas, Sacagawea did what she was told. When she was about twelve years old, she was married to a French-Canadian fur trader. His name was Toussaint Charbonneau. Charbonneau may have paid the Hidatsas for Sacagawea. Or he may have won her in a gambling game. She was probably more of a servant than a wife. She had no idea that she would play one of the greatest roles in American history.

In 1803, the United States bought a huge new territory. It was called the Louisiana Purchase and it doubled the size of the United States. But white Americans knew almost nothing about the new territory. President Thomas Jefferson decided to send a small group of men to explore the new lands and meet the American Indians who lived there. He chose Captains Meriwether Lewis and William Clark to lead the explorers. The group would be called the Corps of Discovery, or the Lewis and Clark Expedition.

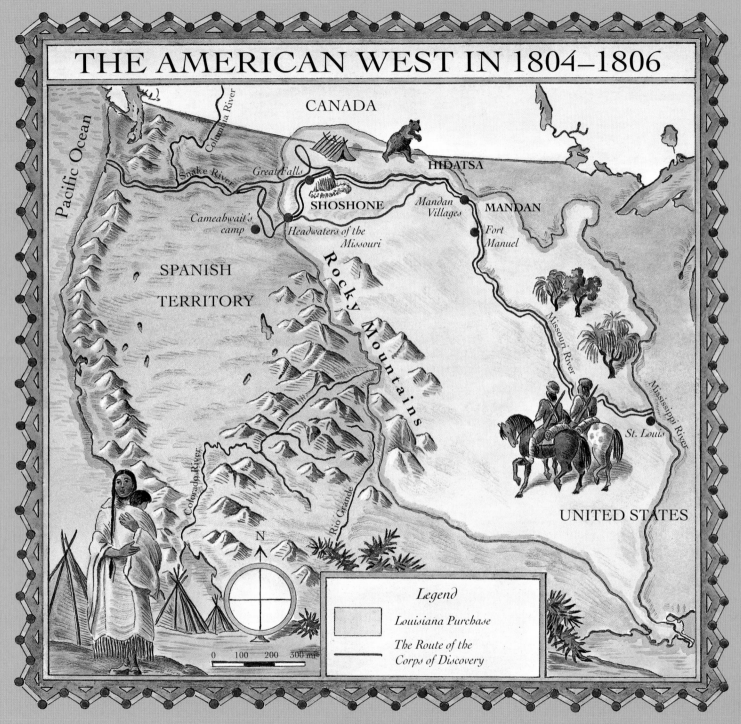

# THE AMERICAN WEST IN 1804–1806

CANADA

Pacific Ocean

Columbia River

Snake River

Great Falls

HIDATSA

SHOSHONE

Mandan Villages

MANDAN

Cameahwait's camp

Headwaters of the Missouri

Fort Manuel

SPANISH

TERRITORY

Rocky Mountains

Missouri River

Colorado River

Rio Grande

Mississippi River

St. Louis

UNITED STATES

N

Legend

Louisiana Purchase

The Route of the
Corps of Discovery

0    100    200    300 mi

*In 1803, Americans knew almost nothing about their
huge new territory of Louisiana.*

*Lewis and Clark spent the winter of 1804–1805 with the Mandan Indians. This is when they met Sacagawea.*

On May 14, 1804, the Corps of Discovery set out from their camp just above the city of St. Louis. In three boats, the men began paddling and pulling themselves up the Missouri River. Within weeks, they started to see bison, grizzly bears, and other amazing animals. By the fall, they reached villages of the Mandan Indians in what is now North Dakota.

The Mandan Indians welcomed the Corps of Discovery. They traded with the explorers and shared meals with them. They allowed them to build a fort to spend the winter in. Hidatsa villages were also nearby. One day, Toussaint Charbonneau and Sacagawea came to visit Lewis and Clark.

Sacagawea was now about sixteen years old, and she was about to have a baby. On February 11, 1805, she gave birth to a boy named Jean Baptiste, or "Pomp." Lewis and Clark decided to hire Charbonneau as an interpreter. Sacagawea and Pomp would come with them.

*Lewis and Clark decided to bring Sacagawea, her husband,*
*and their son on their expedition.*

*Sacagawea's knowledge and bravery soon made her the most valuable member of the Corps of Discovery.*

When spring arrived, the Corps of Discovery again headed up the Missouri River. Sacagawea quickly became one of the most valuable members of the party. One day, she and Pomp were sitting in one of the boats. Suddenly, a blast of wind tipped the boat sideways into the water. Her husband Charbonneau began screaming in fear, but Sacagawea stayed calm. With Pomp tied to her back, she began grabbing trunks and bundles floating in the water. Her courageous act saved important maps, instruments, and other supplies.

In early summer, the expedition spent almost a month dragging their boats around the Great Falls of the Missouri River. Then, they followed the river to its beginnings, or headwaters. It was now almost August. Lewis and Clark worried that they wouldn't be able to cross the Rocky Mountains before winter set in. To cross the mountains, they needed horses from Sacagawea's birth tribe, the Shoshones. The Shoshones, though, were nowhere to be seen.

*To cross the Rocky Mountains, Lewis and Clark
needed horses—and quickly!*

*When Sacagawea saw her people, she was*
*so happy that she cried.*

Sacagawea remembered important landmarks from her childhood. She helped guide Lewis and Clark toward the Shoshones. When Sacagawea saw her tribe, she was filled with happiness. She hugged old friends. Then, she recognized the tribe's chief. It was her brother, Cameahwait! Sacagawea rushed into her brother's arms. Tears streamed down her face.

Over the next few days, the captains bought horses from the Shoshones. Sacagawea was the only person in the expedition who could speak Shoshone. She told her people what the captains wanted. Without her, the expedition probably would have had to turn back. Thanks to her, though, the Corps of Discovery crossed the last of the Rocky Mountains. Finally, in the fall of 1805, the explorers reached the Pacific Ocean.

*Sacagawea was probably the first person from her tribe to see the Pacific Ocean.*

*Lewis and Clark, in a hurry to get home, paddled swiftly down the wide Missouri.*

During their long journey, Lewis and Clark had learned many things about the new lands of the United States. They also proved that there was no easy way to cross by land to the Pacific Ocean.

After spending the cold winter months in the West, they began the long trip back to the United States. By now, Lewis and Clark hurried to get home. Again, they crossed the Rocky Mountains. In canoes, they paddled seventy or eighty miles each day down the Missouri River.

On August 14, 1806, the expedition reached the Mandan villages once more.

Here, Lewis and Clark said a sad good-bye to Charbonneau, Sacagawea, and Pomp. Captain Clark had grown fond of Sacagawea and Pomp. On the return trip, Clark had even named a large rock "Pompey's Pillar" after Sacagawea's son. Clark carved his name and the date into the rock.

*Pompey's Pillar is the only place Captain Clark*
*carved his name during the expedition.*

*When Captain Clark arrived back in St. Louis,*
*he became an instant hero.*

On September 23, 1806, the Corps of Discovery finally arrived back in St. Louis. Lewis and Clark became instant heroes. Their journey opened the way for settlers heading west. But what happened to Sacagawea?

Sacagawea's life after the expedition is almost as mysterious as her childhood. After she left Lewis and Clark, few people wrote anything about her. She and Charbonneau traveled to St. Louis, where they left Pomp with Captain Clark. Captain Clark adopted the boy and made sure he received a fine education.

Some believe that Sacagawea lived to an old age. But most historians think that she died just a few years later. On December 20, 1812, a clerk at Fort Manuel in present-day South Dakota wrote in his journal: "This evening the wife of Charbonneau . . . died of [a] fever. She was a good and best woman in the fort, age about 25."

This woman was almost certainly Sacagawea.

*No one is sure what happened to Sacagawea,*
*but she probably died in 1812.*

*Today, we honor Sacagawea as one of the most important people in American history.*

Sacagawea never knew how important she was to the history of our country. Today, many mountains, rivers, and lakes are named after her. Statues and paintings of Sacagawea can be found throughout the nation. In the year 2000, a new one-dollar coin was issued in her honor. These things remind us of the gifts a brave Shoshone girl gave us two hundred years ago.

# POSTSCRIPT

Although Sacagawea died young, her son Jean Baptiste lived a long, full life. Pomp traveled to Europe with a prince of Germany. Later, he returned to the West. He traveled with his father, Charbonneau, and became a well-known guide and explorer. Many early travelers wrote accounts of this helpful man who was educated and could speak many languages. He probably died in 1866 in Oregon.

Shortly before she died, Sacagawea gave birth to a daughter named Lizette. Captain Clark also adopted her, but what became of her is not known.

Sacagawea's husband, Charbonneau, probably lived into his eighties. He continued to work as a guide, trader, explorer, and gold-seeker. No one recorded when or where he died.

# IMPORTANT DATES

**1788**  Born as a member of the Shoshone people in the northern Rocky Mountains (present-day Idaho and Montana).

**1799 or 1800**  Kidnapped by Hidatsa Indians and taken to present-day North Dakota.

**1800–1803 (?)**  Marries Toussaint Charbonneau, a French-Canadian fur trader.

**1804**  Meets Captains Lewis and Clark of the Corps of Discovery at the Mandan villages in what is now North Dakota.

**1805**  Gives birth to a son, Jean Baptiste, or "Pomp"; joins the Corps of Discovery with husband Charbonneau and son Pomp; reunites with Shoshone tribe; reaches the Pacific Ocean with the explorers.

**1806**  Returns to the Mandan villages with the expedition; says good-bye to Lewis and Clark.

**1807**  Travels to St. Louis with her husband and Pomp; Captain Clark adopts Pomp.

**1812**  Gives birth to a daughter, Lizette.

**1812**  Dies at Fort Manuel in present-day South Dakota.

# WORDS TO KNOW

**bison**  Large mammals that many American Indian tribes hunted for meat and skins; buffalo.

**corps**  A group of people who work together.

**expedition**  A journey made for a special purpose; also, the people going on such a journey.

**explorer**  A person who travels to unknown places to learn about them.

**headwaters**  The small streams that come together to form the beginnings of a river.

**Hidatsa Indians**  A Native American tribe who lived on the Knife River in what is now North Dakota. The Hidatsas were traders and farmers.

**interpreter**  Someone who can speak more than one language and help others communicate with each other.

**Louisiana Purchase**  A huge territory, or piece of land, between the Mississippi River and Rocky Mountains. It was purchased from France in 1803 and more than doubled the size of the United States.

**Mandan Indians**  Friends and neighbors of the Hidatsas. The Mandans lived on the Missouri River in today's North Dakota.

**plains**  Large areas of flat land.

**Shoshone Indians**  A tribe of American Indians living in the West. Sacagawea's band of Shoshones was called the Agaidika, which means "Salmon-Eater Shoshone." The Agaidika lived on both sides of the Rocky Mountains in present-day Idaho and Montana.

**territory**  Any large area of land; a region.

# How to Say It

**Cameahwait**  (kah-ME-uh-wait)

**Hidatsa**  (hee-DAT-sah)

**Jean Baptiste Charbonneau**  (zhaun bap-TEESTE shar-bone-OH)

**Sacagawea**  (sah-KA-gah-WEE-ah)*

**Shoshone**  (shuh-SHOW-nee) or (shuh-SHOWN)

**Toussaint Charbonneau**  (too-SAN shar-bone-OH)

*As you learn more about Sacagawea, you may see her named spelled and pronounced differently. Historians used to think that her name was spelled *Sacajawea* and pronounced sah-kuh-juh-WEE-ah. Today most people think her name was spelled with a *g* rather than a *j*.

# To Learn More about Sacagawea

## WEB SITES

*Public Broadcasting System: Lewis & Clark*
    http://www.pbs.org/lewisandclark
*The Shoshone Indians*
    http://www.shoshoneindian.com
*Sacagawea*
    http://www.sacajaweahome.com
*Official Site of the Fort Lemhi Indian Community*
    http://www.lemhi-shoshone.com/sacajawea.html

## BOOKS

*I Am Sacajawea, I Am York: Our Journey West with Lewis and Clark*
    by Claire Rudolf Murphy. Walker, 2005.

*On the Trail of Sacagawea* by Peter Lourie. Boyds Mills Press, 2001.

*Sacajawea: Her True Story* by Joyce Milton. Grosset & Dunlap,
    2001.

# Index

Page numbers for illustrations are in boldface

# ABOUT THE AUTHOR

**SNEED B. COLLARD III** is the author of more than fifty award-winning books for young people, including *The Prairie Builders*; *A Platypus, Probably*; *One Night in the Coral Sea*; and the four-book SCIENCE ADVENTURES series for Marshall Cavendish Benchmark. In addition to his writing, Sneed is a popular speaker and presents widely to students, teachers, and the general public. In 2006, he was selected as the Washington Post–Children's Book Guild Nonfiction Award winner for his achievements in children's writing. He is also the author of several novels for young adults, including *Dog Sense* and *Flash Point*. To learn more about Sneed, visit his Web site at www.sneedbcollardiii.com.